Sleeping
Through
the
Graveyard
Shift

Al Maginnes

REDHAWK
PUBLICATIONS

Published by Redhawk Publications
2550 US Hwy 70 SE
Hickory NC 28601

ISBN: 978-1-952485-01-5

Cover collage by Sandy Longhorn

Advance praise for *Sleeping Through the Graveyard Shift...*

"Like the workers in his poems - graveyard waitresses, steel men, hot tar roofers - 'whose art is perseverance,' Maginnes the poet always shows up. In poems where a trimmed fingernail means more than the moon, he casts a wary eye on America, but never disowns it. Tempted, he never quite surrenders to pessimism, always just beating the count, rising to the 'voice willing itself to go on,' punching the Poetry card. His 'people' may be 'projects / half-finished,' but he knows that 'monuments rise on the foundations / of failures.' Refusing to believe that 'any love is wrong,' he's Levine-like, a laureate of the lowly, the everyday, and now of late middle-age; a poet who, like his Whitman, finds 'the breaking apart fragments of a universe still beautiful in its mystery.' These are poems you can believe in, you can trust. Poems that are use-full, that can humbly help us 'bear the scars of a day's demands.' There is not much more you can ask of poetry, than that." —Adrian Rice, author of *Hickory Station,* and *The Strange Estate: New & Selected Poems 1986-2017.*

"Like songs on an old record, Al Maginnes' *Sleeping Through the Grave-yard Shift* has the feel of revelation and a call to arms after revelation. They are the captain's log of one who sees past shape-shifting triumph. One after another, these generous-spirited poems treat the reader like a com-plicit friend, like an accomplice or confederate, a coworker-partner who has learned the skill of seeing what needs to be accomplished. The wind-fall change Maginnes spends on jukeboxes and pinball in 'The Day Patty Hearst Was Captured' is currency and passport to a country both fearsome and fervently personal, an America of joy and disappointment and shit-wage transactions that, nonetheless, seem to have the power to redeem. This book is stunning for its many revelations, as in the poem 'Vulture Skull,' where we hear of a 'dark / that hosts both what is foul in us / and any spark of infinity we might own' or in the magnificent final poem 'Hard Luck: A Requiem for Jerry Quarry'—gem-like, the poems open the heart-eye in rooms of light and living shadows. Of course there is music playing. Always-and-forever music."—Roy Bentley, finalist for the Miller Williams Poetry Prize for *Walking with Eve in the Loved City*

Other books by Al Maginnes

Outside a Tattoo Booth
Taking Up Our Daily Tools
The Light In Our Houses
Film History
Dry Glass Blues
Ghost Alphabet
Greatest Hits: 1987-2010
Between States
Inventing Constellations
Music From Small Towns
The Next Place

Table of Contents

1 70 Review: "The Lies Rings Tell" "Fairy Rings"

American Journal of Poetry— "Hard Luck: A Requiem for Jerry Quarry"

Asheville Poetry Review—"Surviving the Storm"

Bookends Review—"Where the Famous Dead Have Fallen"

Chautaqua—"FM DJ's"

Crab Creek Review—"In the Poetry Museum"

Grist—"A Myth of California"

Grub Street—"Contrabands" "My Country"

Hamilton Street Review— "The Day Patty Hearst Was Captured"

Lake Effect—"Vulture Skull"

Meridian—"One Circle"

Mount Hope—"Decanter"

Packinghouse Review—"Fear For What Is Missing"

Platte Valley Review—"Where I Was" "The Chinese Poet Contemplates His Journey"

San Pedro River Review—"The Piano As A City"

Slipstream—"The Next Place Music Might Go"

Steel Toe Review—"District Court As Community Theater"

Sugar House—"Zero Gravity"

ucity review—"Phenomenology" "The Serpent's Faith" "Elephants and Wolves"

Valaparaiso Poetry Review— "Old Records" "The Wax Cylinder: Whitman Reading"

Vox Populi—"Journalism 101"

West Texas Review—"Now That I No Longer Fish"

Wisconsin Review online—"The Gravities of Landscape"

My Country

My country is the billow of breath-steam
flaring from the shotgun-barrel sized nostrils
of a carriage horse in front of the Peabody Hotel.
It is the river that runs treacherous
and full of stories a few blocks west, rolling over
soft crusts of boat hulls, the pitted marbles
of bone. A fishing lure dangles from a branch
thick as a broken finger, a pendulum keeping time
over the small creek. An oil stain on pavement,
a wine bottle shattered to claws of green glass.
My country is lightning on the horizon, thunder
calling long distance, smell of rain like a light beam
over a dark field. It is the lamb led from
the herd, abandoned to the appetite of wolves.
Heedless, it survives and finds its way back
to the tribe. In fall, blood-smeared wool will
be taken. My country is a rock and a breath of wind,
a dream of steel and steel itself. The shaking hand
of a friend who said "I'll be all right" so often
it was clear he would not be. My country is
the light we hid from when we crawled
into culverts to drink warm beer and stare
into a sky until we could pretend
the rip-rap laid down for drainage was a footpath
to lead to the shifting border of the moon.

The Serpent's Faith

The snake made its way out of Eden after it understood
the little nagging behind its eyes would never cease,
never allow him rest. The blame would ride him and him alone
through eternity, no matter how warm the curiosity of the hairless ones,
how deep their appetite. Once the gates vanished
and fruit began to rot on the trees, the other animals
went their ways, seeking their places in a realm
that so far offered only the sound of wind. The ground obeyed
a different nature out here, lay spiked with rocks
and threaded by roots that made motion more difficult.
Grass grew sharp-edged and long. But the snake pushed through,
the spot behind its eyes burning, its body a long muscle
made to skim surfaces like flesh turned to water.
On the fat, sun-scorched rocks or in the root crevices
of trees, rest could be found, far from the snuff-blackened
tongues of grandmothers who repeated tales
of hoop snakes or serpents that broke into separate bodies
and reassembled, all that was need to give staring children
their first fear of sin, verses pulled from the gospel and misquoted
to say this life is but one more skin to crawl out of.

Phenomenology

In Madrid, he bought a pack of Gauloises, spoke a long time
to a woman buying fruit before walking out,

                                            his white suit
shining, his steps precise as a dancer's. In San Francisco
he shuffled a brief buck and wing before a sidewalk band.
Somewhere in Mexico, he received communion, then stopped a vendor
and bought shots of the homemade tequila that made
an encumbrance of the body.

                             Outside Fatima,
the shepherd children who saw the Virgin Mary in 1916
felt the sun slow its immolations long enough
to see a heart glowing clear as the center of a fire
and they heard

                     Mary speak from the deep blank of sky,

                                      making
the children helpless vessels, their old lives spilled,
and all before them blocked by what they'd seen.
It's uncertain

                what happens when the body shrugs and dies
though it seems some stay to dance in white clothes
and others vanish like furniture
abandoned on the curb.

                        While the battlefields
of Europe split with fire, Mary told three frightened,
illiterate children that if her words were heeded,
peace would follow.

                    The man seen on the streets
of half a dozen cities, sported a white linen suit
twirling a gold headed cane,

                        while the body
that had borne him for almost eighty years rested, for once,
still as a stone.

And no one reported any words from him
though he flickered through a handful of afternoons,
the smoke of his last cigarette hovering
in all the last places he was seen.

District Court as Community Theater

Until you understand each role was written
        long before you hit your first mark,
it's easy to smirk at the ill-hanging curtain

of the judge's robe, the "Oyez, oyez," invoking us
        to draw forth and be heard. But when

the finitude of this passion play finally settles
        its ancient weight on your frame,
your hand will linger over the grain

of the Bible's cover, and your eyes will study
        a set not tacked together in shop class:

scuffed wainscoting, dark oil portraits
        of dignitaries smeared into anonymity,
the slow heavy breathing of the man beside you,

half-asleep, waiting, like you, to be called.
        If you believe truth, however thin and shape-shifting,

exists here, you might believe yourself able
        to inhabit any of these roles: grim prosecutor,
insolent defendant, bailiff blinking and stifling a yawn.

You want to deliver your lines with a sense of history's irony,
        your questions and vows punctuated by

a bit of the doubt that salts any human enterprise.
        Only a fool would claim there is no difference
in casting when some slip home to warm meals

11

and the private rest of their beds while others
      chew the cold bologna the country serves on Tuesdays

and twitch in the uneasy sleep of prey.
      Nine hundred dollars or ninety days, sighs the man
beside you, waking as the judge enters and you stand,

a single improvisation before everyone sits, settles
      into rehearsed business, into roles no one owns.

A Chinese Poet Contemplates His Journey

The moon tonight means less than the sliver
        of fingernail I trimmed while I waited

for my wine. To the left of me, wars
        and the stories of wars. From the right,

mythologies and dust. I wish there was
        someone to play music. I would pay

for a song that would help erase all
        that is looming and distant. I wish

I did understand one word I hear
        spoken around me. This purple wine,

this bench where I sit, the sun whose warmth
        lingers, like me, long into evening,

these are all things I hold dear tonight.
        Behind me, a grave. Before me,

another. Soon leaves will whirl
        and die, yellow tongues crisping brown.

The stark penmanship of trees will be written
           against a sky swept bare

as the stones I climbed to the school
           where I learned poems and numbers,

where I learned some roads led
           to the borders of this kingdom,

and some traveled beyond.

America

Like all poets raised in this country trained to breathe
chalk dust, or now the dry marker fumes
of public schools, who stood to pledge allegiance to

the handkerchief-sized flag in the classroom's corner, who
memorized states by classroom rote and inherited
the biases that make our map of this land, I've wanted

to write my ode to America, but she remains a changing target,
neither untarnished as teachers told us or the worm-eaten fruit
the most suspicious among us might claim.

Sometimes when I think of America these days, I recall
the used car where I stood one afternoon, looking deep
into the unknown land of an old engine, seeking the source

of a strange noise I could hear but could not name.
The car I own today couldn't carry me to oceanic forests
or long-extinct herds of buffalo, black as thunderheads,

moving slow as continents across the plain. Now they lie
behind fences. And it's a tricky wicket to tie our dwindling
treecover to a plot to murder the Kennedys or to believe

a GPS administered by vaccine might track us through
every stop in our lives. It's easy to believe you would die
for free speech as long as you can drive to the mall

and order shoes from Amazon. Somewhere, a man with
our flag on his uniform is shooting at another man.
Drones are delivering bombs. A buffalo's tail twitches

at the flies that never stop swarming in summer.
A new history of the Illuminati was just published on the web.
And I remember leaping from the steps of school on the last day.

I knew I could sprain an ankle, tear open a knee. I knew
in a few weeks baseball and the pool would leave me bored shitless.
But for a wild moment, I had freedom to make that long jump

and taste the flowers of exhilaration before I hit the hard ground.

Sacrificing Home

A baseball bat is forty-two inches long
but can carry the right person further
than any outfield can stretch, all the way

from Royston Georgia, known for nearly
nothing, to Chicago, New York, Detroit,
anywhere men and women pay good money

to sit in sun-parched bleachers and watch men
bleed and dirty themselves at a boy's game.
A marriage is a promise, but

it takes only one act to end that promise,
one shot to end it for good. Then a train brings
a boy back from his games to view his father,

visit his mother accused but not arrested for
shooting the man she married when she was twelve.
In the boy's suitcase, the glove he bought

after selling his schoolbooks. And the spikes
his new teammates will watch him sharpen
before his first major league game, three weeks

from tonight. Dark presses the train's windows,
far-off lights flash like pop flies.
Next spring his mother will be acquitted

for shooting the man she claimed she believed
an intruder. Her son will be in Detroit,
already known for giving no quarter when

he runs the bases. The whiskey someone gave him
remains untouched. He needs only the little flask
of rage he uncorks each time he crosses a baseline.

Morning Labor Song

We smoked and drank coffee, talked scores or last night's TV
until light the color of nails started
                              over the trees, moved
slow as the first beading of sweat on the forehead.
What proof that we were intact unless we saw
our shadows
                    shaking in spring cold?
A door opened, then another. Someone took a last swallow
of coffee, someone spit. By the time we walked
onto the job still carrying tools,
                              the chill sun divided us.

And thirty years would pass before I wondered
if that sky, filled with its pale light,
                              held any portion
of the sky I stared into yesterday. All we knew
on those mornings we walked into unmoving cold or heat
implacable as a summons from a judge
                                    was that a sky would
watch us and one day see us fall.

Tonight the distant winding of sirens,
                        Night stitched
from a thousand pieces of cloth. Windows blink dark,
locks assert themselves in doors. But car engines catch,
speakers cry their cold anthems.
                        A few solitaries
turn pages or stare at stars
                        which have no sequel,
no final page. When the show is over, the sky rolls blank.
But the workers always show up, hefting cold tools,

19

walking out like their first task is to tear down
the scaffolding needed to construct another night's sky.

Now That I No Longer Fish

water has retreated into
older mystery. I have
no need to clarify
the length and shape
of shadows cruising
below the brackened faces
of ponds. But the three quarters
of my body made from
water draws me to scan
the dark barriers, their echoes
of a time when what came
to land was neither fish
nor mammal, but half-creatures
seeking the element
that fit best. Only later
would that choice disappear.
The borders of land and water
made themselves, and once made,
dissolve only in dreams
without beginning or end,
only the mirage of shadows
underwater, small deceptions
reminding us how all
that entices can also kill.

A Treatise on Art: Why I Don't Read Science Fiction

We were promised the moon before the first
          footprints of men violated that dust, when
it was simply a blank orb, hung there for the taking.
          Then would come Mars, winking red dot,
where civilizations had been conjured by generations
          of writers facing inevitable gravities
of rent, liquor, alimony, the galaxy of bills
          that empties an honest pocket. Beyond Mars,
the stars still being named, new planets shining
          in their fields, building incandescent belts.

The stars were facts as much as the microbes
          the third grade science book said were hovering
in the graphite of my pencil, sulking deep
          in the wrinkles of my shirts, universes
too small to measure. This was all the science I knew
          when I went to see a movie with
my friend up the street and his mom. The movie told
          a story about the earth splitting in half.
I chafed in my cushioned chair, clueless
          as the scientists trying to understand
how near the end was. I'd hit the ground enough
          in backyard football games, fallen from trees
enough to know how solid earth's surface is.

From the start my curiosity reserved itself for
          things that had proven true and would prove
their mystery again. The choreographies of *Star Trek*
          owned no enchantment for me. But the unexplored
galaxies, the radiant bodies of some girls
          I was starting to notice were worth a million

burning stars or collapsed planets. I swallowed a hit
of cheap acid to see the first *Star Wars* movie,
but never saw the sequels and prequels that built
a universe whose gravity was money.

In my forties, mid-life sounded voids
in my knowledge, and I began reading about
the universe, enough to get schooled in a few
age-old conundrums—Heisenberg's theory,
Schrodinger's cat, and I learned that some notions
I'd believed the province of hungover pulp writers,
wormholes in space and time, parallel universes,
hidden dimensions—are, for some physicists
working theories. Now every week uncovers

some new fact or question casting doubt on everything
we think we know about the universe, new galaxies,
an Earth-like planet it would take 400 human lifetimes
to reach. Maybe we are living inside
the last science fiction novel. But the ground holds
solid beneath our feet so we can stare
into the little hollows of our phones, each
more powerful than the room-sized computers
of the 1970s. And the universe goes on unraveling
around us, making each star not elegy
but an editor's mark, shrinking creation to the size
of a screen, a page too small to know
how the story gets written or how it ends.

Love In Vain

For DB

If we could make mixtapes for those departed
into the silence of the afterlife, there would never be

room enough to include all the music necessary,
and I'd be left to curse the song I'd deprived

some friend or loved one from hearing throughout
the long aftermath. Tonight I'm thinking of "Love In Vain,"

the one song by Robert Johnson I can't find
mentioned in your book of the blues. For half an hour,

I've switched between the dust-born noise
of Robert Johnson's version and the rendition offered by

The Rolling Stones on *Get Your Ya-Yas Out.* More time
has passed since the Madison Square recording

than between Johnson's first recording and the Stones' cover.
Johnson sounds weary as a bad year as he watches

his baby leave on the train for Lethe or some shade-tangled
branch of the underworld. Two lights, one red, one blue,

burn from the back of that vanishing train, a glow
to turn all desire to ash. The electric slide drawl

of Mick Taylor's guitar, Mick Jagger's fatback enunciations
that never quite erase London make the woman metaphor

for the desire of these men to tune and chord the black dirt,
the hangman's moon, all the sweet voodoo of the blues.

The Stones' baby, though, is not bound for hell, but London,
Manchester, Brawley, somewhere time-locked and sensible,

unlike Johnson's lover, whose fate lingers between the drawn-out
notes the guitar can reach, the crackle of dust like time unfolding.

I wish those lights, red and blue, had been enough to vanish
the anger that rose between us and silenced correspondence

during your last months, when it was still possible
for you to hear those songs and remake them in the alchemy

of your poems. I don't believe any love is wrong, even
the ones that hurts us empty, that makes us moan

like a piece of metal slurring down the neck
of a guitar. I don't believe there is any song

that is not a yearning for something else. We are
creatures made restless with desire, forever riding away

or waving farewell, always believing
a stranger will descend from the dark platform,

take our tired arms, ask our names, convince us
that once, at least, love will not be in vain.

FM DJ's

Vanished like dollar meals,
two for one happy hours, like
forty cent gas, night herons
and Carolina parakeets, gone
like true believers, the men
and women whose voices, rich
as whole notes, drew
smoke-shadows through bedrooms
of solitary teenagers across
half a state. Because they chose
the songs they played, at least
once a night the still air rang
rich with the communion
of surprise, rhyming chords
that could bring the life
I was not living, that none
of us was living, into view
and make it seem possible,
the stars suddenly closer
for the minutes the song lasted,
all I wanted burning
into plain sight if I could
only find a way to reach it.

Who listening did not want,
at least once, to be them,
did not fall briefly in love
with them, even though, seen
in person they disappointed?
They were, finally, voices,
human variations on the tubes

Victorian ladies spoke through
calling for biscuits and tea,
ordering the carriage brought round,
technology flown the way of
the imperial woodpecker, the red-
throated woodrail. But if
they were conduits for sound,
they knew another message as well,
their silence signal for our own
when they put on an album
and let it play straight through.

They had to know as they dropped
the needle on *Thick as a Brick*
or *Cactus Live!* how brief
their time would be, how soon
the glassy soliloquies
about Watkins Glen or Sabbath
on their first American tour
would be muffled by those
willing to work from playlists,
who were never silent, talking
over each song's opening
and into the first verse,
who wanted audiences trained
to be happy hearing the same
twenty songs day after day.

Like the passenger pigeons
whose great flocks once covered
the sun, one year they were
everywhere, each city sporting
its own hip station. Then
they were vanishing, then gone.

I pay for the music
I listen to now, so I know
what song is coming next.
No worries about reception.
No surprise, no riff I waited
all night, waited without knowing
I waited, to hear. No names
of bands disappearing
into songs heard once and vanished
before I could forget I heard them.

Ghost Crabs

Because the afterlife bears mystery
this dirt will not sustain, we learn
a new name for these armored crawlers
with their claws and briny scowls.
My daughter and her friend scrape
along the lacy surf line with a bucket
and small shovel, searching for
those burrowing nocturnals. They laugh
into wind that blows the sound away.
Tomorrow my daughter will be twelve.
Tonight she is content searching for
sand crabs--now ghost crabs--, beings
content to exist without us. In a few years
the joyous hazards of night
will arrive in dark cars, chrome
gleaming like blades, in the insincere
handshakes of boys I will never quite like
or trust, in all the temptations
I would take on for her if I could.
But she must dig into that dark sand
with her own hands, see for herself
the small, fierce things of night.
But that is a wave that has yet to break.
Tonight I'm pleased to peer into
her bucket, her cupped hands and see
the small, untamed life she holds.

Dark History

The sky, we praise always. The bones, never.
The plains and deep mountains sketched glories
we were told to worship. Never the crow.
Never the trickster beast. The eagle would
be our talisman. All written for us.
We could ignore the death songs bodies must
give in tribute to our circle of flesh.
The dirt, the grass, all earth was ours to take.
This was the myth that seasoned us. Rivers,
trees, coal would be infinite forever.
We could laugh at those who thought such things holy.
Whatever we restored would be reborn
as we secretly thought we would be.
Possibility would remain endless
for hands made to receive and shape the sky,

We Live On What We Bury

The dirt has not aged by any measure you can read,
      but the landscape has shifted, grown fragile

in the blink of decades since you last drove this town
      where the first slow dance, the paralyzing virgin drag

on a cigarette remain, bargain items in a pawnshop
      that sells memory's bric a brac. Recall skin pulsing

against your nervous hand, the black grave going wide
      as you choked for air, then raised

the cigarette for that second draw. Slow inventory says
      what buildings have grown in lots once given

to oak or yellow-tipped pine. The boy who lived in your body
      back in those shade-cloaked days, walked sidewalks

buckled as the teeth in his mouth, listening for notes
      between clouds, for bones left for centuries under

sleeping dust, dirt that sees the fall of houses, dirt dug
      and pushed into mounds to make room for construction,

piles for boys to climb with a determination that stops time.
      If that boy saw you today, slow-cruising your memory,

would he believe even once he could be you, steering the past,
      deaf to the song bones and dirt make of time?

The Gravities of Landscape

When my wife got the phone call about her friend's death,
I was reading an interview with her hometown sheriff
who lamented the swampy mess a ruined meth lab had made
of one more house and lot, this one a place he loved to visit
as a boy and hates to look at now, he says.
I've driven by the same house on a road just outside
the town where my wife grew up. Fields blend into fields,
brown sprawls barely separated by stark ranks of pine.
I always slow down driving there, pleased by the wide view
of sky, the way the road's long curves fool me into believing
I have no special place to be. Houses and their outbuildings
seem tiny, like the houses and hotels my sister and I crowded
onto Boardwalk and Atlantic on Saturday mornings when
we stale-mated at Monopoly, neither able to accumulate
enough to wipe the other out. A bulldozer will knock
the house flat; men in hazmat suits will haul away debris,
then scour the very dirt before they are sent to the wreckage
of another lab, one set up last night or tonight,
now basting the air with its blend of low-riding chemicals.

I have never loved or hated any landscape.
By fifteen I had visited too many places, lived
in too many houses not to understand the neutrality
of setting. Once, on a back porch overlooking
an ocean, I lay in a hammock and slept so long
my wife came to see if I had slipped, smiling,
into coma or death. I knew a man who returned
to his hometown for a funeral and, on a whim,
walked into the high school where, thirty years before,
he was voted Most Likely to Succeed. He nearly wept
at seeing how small the classrooms were, how narrow

the broom-swept halls, how much of the place he still carried
after thirty years. Death might remove the landscape
we know, but time's gentle gravity will pull
all we do know flat. I have driven that road, but was never
there to inhale the fumes of cooking speed drifting
like waves of yellow pollen the pines release each spring.
I never saw the toothless and tweaking customers pacing circles
under a 4 a.m. moon, trying to catch the breath
that fluttered just in front of them. I've forgotten
or haven't said that the inevitable end of the games we played
Saturday mornings was a hand sweeping the board into ruin—hotels,
houses, stubborn dice on the floor. My wife's friend is dead.

Still the sky divides and is whole again. Somewhere,
another board is populated for a round of Monopoly
of risk. Tractors froth through dirt, dust clouds and diesel smoke
in their wake like scavenger birds. I would even claim hope
in the endless cat and mouse of the meth cooks and the cops,
each hide and seek, each discovery a move in a larger game.
And if I find hope in that circling, I can believe
in the little angels rising, restless, from country graves
to move toward low-burning flames, the smell of desire,
addicted to the fumes and to the purity
of one drug-riddled boy who hopes with each breath
for rest, rest one angel would gladly provide if only
it was possible for angels to assume flesh and its landscapes,
its complications of landscape that are endless
as the dirt flesh rises from, only to spend
a life resisting the gravity of inevitable return.

Letter to Logan

I discovered you inside
Hugo's letter poem, an ode
to intemperance and mortality,
a message from one ex-drunk
to another. "Piss on sobriety,"
Hugo writes, and even at 19,
I had some notion I might
one day receive a like message:
"As drunks we're done." But
drunks rarely are done. There is
always a reason for celebration
or sorrow or just because, for
"this, just one more"
as Jimi Hendrix wrote.
You probably heard Hendrix
seeping through bar talk
or under the noise of a party
where poets spilled drinks
and gossip, where a woman kissed
a man she wasn't married to.
All for love or art.
I went to that party. More
than once. It goes on
somewhere tonight.
But not for me. And not
for you either, lost to the sure
and certain grave. Now
what I wonder is when I will
ever be done with drinking.
Not the drink itself—that glass
emptied years ago—but the myth

that keeps me writing about it,
retelling the same stories
the way Keith Richards jokes
about the heroin he gave up
decades ago. Hendrix, Richards,
you can read my romance with
the regalia of doom, the musicians
crossed and cursed by the moon,
the poet consumed by shadows.
I send these missives out
to the unmet and unknown,
as though I might scrawl
a bridge between here and the place
you went, as if one day
I might look where my hand has been
and see an answer for myself,
written plain for any who
believe enough to ask.

Contrabands

It could be a book, a bottle of smuggled liquor, cigars or seeds forbidden

       to carry across the borders invisible

below the wings of the plane. It could be the tracts of some faith, hidden

       and ancient, one that condones

sacraments not spoken of under certain flags. It could be a laptop stuffed

       with the secrets of a collapsed economy

nested inside pictures of butterflies and soccer players. There are gun parts,

       designs stolen from dressmakers bound

for the runways of London and Cannes, impossible fragments dripping

       from the human scaffolding of models

trained not to speak and to move with the grand selfishness of cats. You know

       the laws of your land forbid the blue liquor,

but a few sips turn you visionary at last, and you could not leave such insight

       stranded in a republic where

you could only ask what something cost and how long before the arrival

       of the train, dialogue

that turned to ash when a few sips from a thick glass set free a flutter

       of swallows, wings speeding

between brain and heart, a tumult to cast a glittering over all you saw.

So you built a lair deep in your luggage to store two bottles, determined

       to bring the sight

of near-prophecy home with you. But even the hangover of insight

       will not whisper what rests

in the suitcase next to yours. The thick-set man sleeping in his seat across the aisle, a strand

of spit silver in his beard, believes the old scripture he unburied in

a bookstore tucked deep

in the elbow of a back street contains all the knowledge he has waited

his entire conscious life to learn.

Soon he will build the pillowy dome of his heaven, will witness perfection

he has been told does not exist.

This is how it is for travelers, each of us bearing at least one secret,

one small treachery forward

among dirty socks, wrinkled shirts. But the young man, dreamless and twitching

in the seat beside

the fugitive historian, consults his watch, counts backward again. His device

has failed and now

his manifesto of martyrdom, flashing on screens across the world, means nothing.

Arrest, the humiliation

of trial and captivity. Tonight, you will come home, pour glasses of contraband

liquor for your wife and you,

and as your sight and breathing expand, the iron fear that seized you when

the young man was pulled from

the line in front of you will dissolve and you will tell your wife

about the door he vanished through,

one you never knew existed, and how you and your fellow travelers

were left

to claim whatever secrets you managed to keep hidden for now.

Decanter

Because my sister said not to,
        because I wanted to mark the quiet

with some motion, I lifted
        the faceted bottle and peered

through it to see my grandmother's den
        divide into angles and shapes,

walls bending inward, then receding.
        Then I made her look. If we could

divide the room into fractions, it was
        one more way to split the hours

our parents were gone, our grandmother
        busy at tasks we could not help with.

When I raised the decanter higher
        and peered through the liquid,

the distortions of a moment before swirled
        in a brown wash, tincture of nicotine,

reminder that in a few hours, the adults
        of the family would sit here to smoke,

to drink from this bottle, all of them
        talking at once. I pulled the glass stopper,

inhaled the thin, hard smell, blend

of earth and chemistry, element burning

element down to something hot, regretful.
       I did not taste it. Not yet.

I placed the bottle back and time stilled
       once more, a wash of motion thin

and invisible as the liquid settling
       back down the walls of a container

older than I was that afternoon.

My People: A Citizen's Report

My people will not stop the song just because
      strings break. They are cars left in the rain

with the windows down. Strands of wire stripped
      of insulation. We do not clap in rhythm or sing along

at concerts. We dance at home with our partners,
      unseen. We have floorboards filled with cans

to be recycled. Checks torn in half to be
      written again. My people are believers

who will not speak their prayers aloud.
      They vote but will not tithe. They live reckless

and slow. We believe an eagle's shadow
      is a blessing. My people are projects

half-finished. Plank and cinderblock shelves of books
      waiting to be read one day when time stops pushing us

to the time clock, the nine to five when the broken watch,
      long buried, yields to an afternoon's tinkering.

And we take a slow step from our front steps into time,
      one more tribe flowering out of, then falling

into history, whose other name is dust.

Surviving the Storm

Heavy cavalry. The wind a herd
                              of restless gray horses
stampeding the trees. Grapeshot barrages of rain
spangle windows,
                    lend distance and beauty
to the weather outside.
                          Leaves sail from branches,

tumbling casualties of storm. The streets themselves
empty in all this motion, fraying rain,
wind determined to find us where we hide.

            *   *   *

Years, decades, the tree's center
dampened from within,
                      a decay
slow and invisible, fibery heart softened
to punk wood, something between liquid
and solid. Unburnable.

Yet it held. Till now.
                        Till this storm,
spinning inland from the coast, pulls
at the shell of wood-flesh, finds
tendons ready to crack,
                          muscles
no longer able to stay upright.

It would fall
                from the neighbor's yard

41

into ours, the noise lost
in the pitch of storm,
                  erasing
property lines.
             We looked outside
to find the disruption we felt
more than we heard,
                  just as the house
went dark,
          leaving us
undistracted, swelling inside
every weakness we call home.

         *   *   *

In my twenties, one more construction job.
A guy on the crew, someone
I didn't know well
             asked
if we had a room to rent.
                The night before
a car hit its horn at 2 a.m.,
a drinker coming home from the bars,
and his roommate rolled out of bed
screaming, "Take cover,"
               then fired
two shots out the window.

The week before he'd found the same roommate
naked in the yard during a rainstorm.
"Vietnam," he said, "fucked his head up."

         *   *   *

When it was feared that a century's turn
would knock out electricity
                              long enough
to collapse the memorized codes
of civilization,
                    some stored food,
ammunition. And some of those battalions
of tuna, canned fruit, and vegetables
still wait
            like the cans we found
in a barn behind an old farmhouse once.
With a pocketknife, we peeled open
a rusted can of pears,
                            but would not
eat one or taste its juice.
                              Years after
the wars have moved elsewhere,
children still find cannonballs
and mortar shells half-buried
in fields and riverbeds, their poison
sealed in a pocket of rust.

            *   *   *

What part of the body steers toward
its own destruction? At the end,
the soured core of the tree uttered
the prayer it was capable of,
desire to be taken quickly,
a dying body's lament
                        at how slowly
destruction comes.
                    And then the fall.

43

     *   *   *

One night, years before the storm
that knocked over the neighbor's tree,
                    I drove
the fringes of bad weather, racing
tornado warnings to get home.
              Heat lightning made
silhouettes of trees and houses,
                lit the low and rolling
bellies of clouds.
          The radio rattled
with its own storm, voices gusting
blame and vitriol,
            talking to convince themselves
their hatred was earned,
             as if the slow erosion
of rot was not rooted in their words.

     *   *   *

His roommate was quiet most of the time,
he said
        as we shoveled gravel.
Had a good job, didn't party much.
But sometimes things—
           you never knew what—
set him off and he was back
in Nam again.
         "I missed that war.
I don't want it to kill me now."
He let his shovel lean,
           turned
from the wind to light a smoke.

      *   *   *

The next morning,
             silence.
Leaves scattered like ballots
uncounted and cast away.
               Power lines
in the dirt, crippled snakes, their venom
dried for now, ropes that bound nothing.
Dumb pools of water made streets
impassable,
         their dark faces holding
the glare of ragged sky.

But no words, no radio speech for
all that was broken around us.

      *   *   *

First the slow-tilting
           in rain-softened earth,
an imbalance brewed down through years.
The first cracks, splinter-thin,
adding up to a larger breaking.
             The noise
of artillery, sound that silences everything
around it.
      Then a deeper groan,
a sigh of old defeat,
           uttered deep
in the tree's hollowing center.

The whole body falling,

              like a man,
an empire, the collapse
                  coming
for half-a-century and done in seconds.

        *   *   *

A noise that shakes
                    a dozen men from sleep,
their hearts firing, bodies shivering
beneath a skin of sweat.
Old tracer fire, old wounds.
Old blood that never learned to heal.

        *   *   *

Drawn once by the awful and common
news of a shooting at a school,
I watched with everyone else and saw an old friend
walk out of a building
                    wiping her eyes,
speaking the half-formed language
survivors understand.

        *   *   *

When the rot that swallows
the cracked trunk of the tree's republic
sets its claws,

        when it spreads enough
that the body falls to time and gravity,

how long will we trace the snarl
of roots torn from the dirt-womb
and splayed before us

        until
we understand that what killed the tree
did not invade. It was born there.

Fear For What Is Missing

I fell asleep watching a game I cared nothing about,
woke long after midnight in the blue flicker
of the TV screen, cold equivalent of campfires

where I once unrolled my sleeping bag. In one of those
movies meant to make us believe the world is both
crueler and simpler than we imagine, a woman weeps

for her missing child. My mistake is watching
long enough to become tangled in the story, to place myself
among the ex who has fled with the child, the stoic friend,

the intrepid detective crossing state lines, breaking rules,
fracturing procedure, always a step behind. And the mother
who seethes and wails through her scenes, crumpling into pockets

of anguish before each commercial break. After
I turn off the TV, after I walk to my daughter's room
to make sure she is breathing, there is nothing

but to lie there and wait for sleep, the long rush of tires
on the road, the distant noise of sirens either a promise
that no part of this world is safe or an insulation holding

all those undreamt hazards at bay. And lying there,
I remember something else: tonight my friend who lives
as far from me as it's possible to get and still be

in this country plans to ask the woman he loves
to marry him. Because love begets fear, because lately
so many friends have crashed and burned, because they are new

to each other, I worry for them. But last month,
their faces swam with hope, half-liquid in the candle-shimmer
of a restaurant kept dim to give each table an illusion

of privacy though we had to walk sideways, bumping chairs,
murmuring "Excuse me" all the way to the door. Already,
their talk was laced with the small paths, the locks

and hidden codes couples construct, code forgotten
by the couple on TV who swear hot revenge
and slam down phones. The more nights I watch my daughter

sleep or hold her when she cries awake from a dream
she won't remember, the less I am able to watch movies
about the one missing. Fear rushes to fill empty spaces,

arriving one-minded and nameless as love for my daughter
or when I wake curled around my sleeping wife. But I have been
awake too long. Giving up on sleep, I turn on the TV, just in time

to see mother and child reunited, hugging so tight
their embrace seems to promise that scars are one more myth,
another bad dream. The husband, still snarling, is handcuffed,

The screen goes dark for a moment. I hope, on the other side
of the country that my friends did not watch this movie, that they sleep
or lie together, her new ring somehow bright,

even in the now-quiet shadows. I hope they fear nothing.

One Circle

Maybe you are the one who stays awake all night
        stitching the rage and grief of absence

into a shirt you can wear, its colors dark and bright
        as wounds. Maybe you are the neighbor who wakes

to the bone-coughing rattle of an engine's stutter
        into motion, who checks the time and realizes

it's the weekend. A few more hours to sleep. Or maybe
        you are the tire tearing a pocket of gravel

or the gravel itself, chocking the underside of the car,
        then falling, roadside dust settling where you fell.

You could be the dust, pervasive as breath,
        and you would wonder, if you were capable

of wonder, why anyone leaves in such a hurry.
        The dog that jumped the fence last night

sniffs roadside dust, doesn't worry about cars
        or stray humans. And the dog's owner, searching,

calls out his window, slow drives the streets
        near your house, moving in wider circles,

dread slowly coloring each syllable he calls.
        But you are the one who left your house, who drives

sleepless, eyes fogged and burning, shaking against

what cannot be said. She is gone.

You don't know where. Or why you are driving this fast.
      Do you feel the thump or hear it? The dog falls.

The back tire passes over him, presses the last air
      from his body. Then you are

the last breath, dissolving molecules that will
      gather to become the choked cry

of the man who finds the dog, one useless syllable
      of grief and brimstone,

almost enough to awaken the sleepy
      and indifferent god who rolls on his side,

half aware of a new sorrow, one more fracture
      he can't repair. Sleepless for centuries,

he lies on his back, eyes closed to all
      the sorrow and anger he invented

but never received apology for.

The Next Place Music Might Go

No one said *percussion* when we slapped hands against our thighs

       and chests, trying for the jivetime rhythm called hambone,

bodies the first drums humans learned, before the rattle of bones

       or fingers on skin stretched and dried. When the moon was a silent god

and horns and strings were accidents waiting to be discovered,

       to be tamed into the scripture of melody and counterpoint.

When each shift of sky was a song without accompaniment.

       But we knew nothing of percussion's history, learned hambone

from *Hee Haw,* a show hard to find now in the patternless web

       of cable and satellite, a program so clownish it became

one of the few things my whole family laughed at. Ignorant

       of the talking drums forbidden by slave masters, we slapped

our deaf and awkward bodies when teachers' backs were turned,

       interested more in foolishness than rhythm. I have written of music

so often I wonder what is left to say, until a note, a drum fill reminds me

       music lives inside the body, neighbor to hunger and desire,

a part of me as much as the sleepy fog that wraps my spine in late afternoon

      or the calf muscle whose cramps sometimes shock me awake.

When John Coltrane stopped playing his horn, when he began to pound

      his chest and sing a wordless chant into the mike at a concert

recorded in 1966, he was seeking truth of sound, the body's promise

      to resonate when layers of theory have fallen away, when

breath and rhythm build their own circle, each seeking

      the next place music might go.

The Wax Cylinder: Whitman Reading

No human voice could hold in such black clay, even allowing for the passage of time, the breath-shortened hills and gravel-floored valleys of the human voice needled into soft wax and saved. What you hear is the dust-crackle and white noise hiss, the span of years collapsing between our vigil here and Whitman, a quilt over his lap, a cat rolling in the parallelograms of light slanting through the windows while Whitman reads or recites "America" into the unnamed and unlistening void we call time.

When I was young, still too green to be one of the young men whose bathing Whitman celebrates, my sister and I cut cardboard discs from the backs of cereal boxes and played them on the boxy record player we shared, pretending we did not hear the static, the crunch of the needle grinding the shallow grooves, so we could hear The Archies or The Honey Bees singing through a moment when music seemed ready to take over the world.

However recording has changed, the sound of the voice and our fascination with capturing it has not. We love hearing what is said or sung, whether it is carved like a hieroglyph into wax or pressed into a scrap of memory deep in the wiring of a computer, where Whitman's voice is one click of information, poor vessel for the going-away words of a man who believed language could unite or at least name all the breaking apart fragments of a universe still beautiful in its mystery.

The Lies Rings Tell

I don't know what became of the ring after the divorce.
There was no money to be gotten for it since the attempt to pawn it

only proved my promise was worth nothing. No truly grand gesture—
flinging it into the endless surge of the Mississippi, burying it

in a jar with a note or poem, dropping it in a shot of whiskey—seemed
worth the effort. Fog stitches around the trees, drops silent as a web

to hide the hard elbows in the road, the low branches that claw
throats and eyes. A boy learns again the lunacy of fishing with

a naked hook. But better out here with this silent water
and even these unresponsive fish than in the drum-locked hostility

of his parents' house. Walking home, he thinks something shines
in front of him on the road. One night, when he had been sitting

in one spot for a long time, the moon, so thin that barely a whisper
of cold light stuttered down from it, he saw four deer,

their bodies more shadow than flesh, come to the water
to drink. The largest raised its head to sniff the air, the way he does

coming in the door after a long absence, trying to read what might happen.
From the asphalt he picks up a scratched circle of metal, too large

for his fingers, but something he decides to keep, a promise
of the day he won't have to hide in the place he lives.

Journalism 101

A friend stops me in the headache-dim
      florescence of the hall that houses
our little hive of offices to say she liked
      a record review I wrote for
a website that published it without
      letting me know, her words
a soft echo of the cymbal-laden overtures
      I once half-expected each time
I got in print. "I guess you'll be leaving
      now that you're making money
on your writing," she joked, and the eclipse
      on her face from joking
to disbelief saddens me as I explain
      21st century Grub Street, where
success is measured not in readers
      or the quality of the writing
or even dollars, but in mouse clicks.

There are writers—I've shaken their hands,
      stood-sentry still beside them
in elevators—who do get checks
      large enough to cover a month's rent
or take the family to the beach
      for a week for writing a piece
on baseball or learning to tie a Windsor knot
      by watching their dads. In 1977,
I was a college freshman, writing
      for my school newspaper at thirty five cents
a column inch. My market value has
      eroded since then, though not my worry
at being chased down by someone

I interviewed and quoted incorrectly.
In those post-Watergate years,
    no one wanted to be taped, leaving me
to scribble as the subjects of my stories talked,
    trying for something like the words
they said without thinking. I missed words,
    the occasional phrase, sometimes
whole sentences. Has there ever been
    an administrator without the gift
of talking while saying nothing? One afternoon
    I left a dean's office after listening
for forty-five minutes to an explication
    of the thinking behind a new parking lot

and knew I never wanted to write any words
    built only on the dry sand of facts
and economics. Not when the great pillars
    of clouds supported the sky. The shifting
ceilings of leaves offered refuge for any
    words wandering the alleys or perched
on corners of the ramshackle neighborhood
    where my vocabulary dwelt. A place
to watch traffic tangle and pass while
    I made plans that blew away like
silent syllables of cigarette smoke. I can't
    abandon that neighborhood, but long ago
abandoned the idea of making any money
    on my sonnet cycle built on the numerology
of forgotten tribes or the blank verse detective novel
    I've threatened but never found a plot for
or the desire to actually do the thing. So
    I keep writing books that won't find
their way into airports. But I won't have to face
    the nervous ghost of myself from 1977,

scribbling what he hopes are the correct words,
  dreading my shadow in the hall when
I come, demanding payment for
  inaccuracies he was not paid to write down.

Elephants and Wolves

In stories meant to frighten us into obedience, it was wolves
        slinking across snowy pages into the shadow-smothered

night jungles of our rooms. When he was four, my brother would wake
        screaming that elephants were stampeding his room.

That lasted until my father took him to a zoo and let him see elephants
        for the first time. Years before, when I was five or six.

my father took my sister and me to a small circus where you were allowed
        to feed the elephants. One stretched its wrinkled trunk

to take the peanut I held and blew a spray of wet dust across the chest
        of my new white T shirt. I remember crying over the shirt,

but no abiding fear of elephants. When I saw a wolf for the first time,
        it was in a pen and barely the size of a large dog.

Not the predator who feasted on grandmothers and little pigs.
        It's what we can't see that wakes us, that trembles

in our blood and waits patiently for a name.
        When I stopped drinking, a strange landscape opened shapeless

before me, its inhabitants built mostly from shade. A terrain that turned
        treacherous the afternoon a doctor said I had hepatitis C.

Now animals I couldn't see, animals too dark for any zoo prowled
        the back trails of my blood. One by one, the nights not drinking

added to each other, giving my life a shape unexpected
   and filled with silvery creatures that flew close, each

bearing a feather-weight of sun. Then came the storm-cloud wings
   of hep C and the tumult of medications

that hollowed my body until I felt my bed-shaped grave open
   below me. Years of wolves and elephants.

Until the late autumn day my doctor, in her coat white
   as the shirt I wore that day at the circus said

the last medicine did its job, the predators in my blood had vanished,
   smoke over the hills. Last week's rain dowsing a camp's remains.

Things still frighten me. Unexplained pain. Fear of not being able
   to protect the ones I love. Fear I don't know

well enough to name. Wolves. Elephants. And I recall
   childhood's story of the five blind men trying to learn

what an elephant is —an infinity of shapes we only know
   parts of, the rest left to imagination and silence

where wolves grow long teeth and plot ways to ruin
   the shining clothes we wear to deny their presence.

Fairy Dust

After my daughter and her friend filled a mesh-fine bag
       with glitter and called it fairy dust, we found

those flakes everywhere for a few days, winking from
       tabletops, book covers, shining out of the little piles

of dust and dog hair we sweep from the room's far reaches,
       their gleam an emblem of imagination's hold

as they change tables into castles, chairs into horses,
       our hapless dog into a dragon. Once,

after a reading, some of us drove
       to the liquor store before we went to the party,

an event often more anticipated than the reading
       (and with good reason). But tonight had been different.

The reader had opened that place language sometimes will,
       his words angling the world with new light. Someone said

he felt he should be home writing and we nodded.
       "But here we are," I said as we parked in front

of the liquor store. We were as shining as angels then,
       each holding a full measure of the bright dust

that could slip us past the apprenticeship of pre-dawn
       and post-midnight scribbling, of writing books

we would throw away, the years of bad jobs and rejections.
      Wrapping night-clouded fingers around brown bottles

of beer, it was the glory of tomorrow we tasted. Tonight,
      I made the mistake of watching candidates for office debate,

each working to sprinkle the crowd with his own toxic glitter.
      We all believe in some form

of cheap miracle, of transformation that takes nothing.
      I had no idea how many years of work waited for me

when shadows darked the dull moons of my hands
      outside Dickson Street Liquors that night and how,

thirty years later, these little scales still
      spark my hands even after I wash them clean.

A Myth of California

Those who have encountered foxfire
      testify to the beauty available in decay.
One man, eyes sharp with witness, said
      he believed now there are places
the bony wings of angels brush this firmament.
      But he held his fingers from that glowing,
content to watch one world ending
      where another, larger, unknown, began.

Some beauty, like ripples of gold
      in a prospector's pan, can ignite greed,
but a beauty that arrives as a summons
      from the other side of existence,
fire so fragile it signals its own extinction,
      makes us desire myth, not substance.
Lately California, itself on fire, might be myth.
      Every message I've sent burns unanswered.

Where I grew up California was the place
      one went for a final reckoning.
You returned, bronzed in glory
      or battle torn, bearing scars
that are, for some, another kind of beauty.
      Or you never came back, the means
of passage most certain to place you among
      myths of the consumed or disappeared.

Myth or not, I have stood transfixed
      at the line between what is beautiful
and what is destroyed—fire flowering
      from upper story windows, pulse of lights

around a late night accident. The future
in California was the future anywhere—
work, a deck of monthly bills, slow gratitude
for sunsets and quiet music.

The lure was proximity to the tryst
or possible tryst of beauty and ruin,
glamour enough to pull countless
visionaries from the south or Midwest
bearing easels and guitars. Some became citizens.
Others still search, or, like me, had it out
with beauty and ruin, time's assertions
over matter, someplace other than California.

Where the Famous Dead Have Fallen

For Dixon Boyles

In his wallet, Dixon kept his ticket to the concert Lynyrd Skynyrd was flying to when the plane crashed. When he was home from college he used to ride with his friends to the field where Rick Nelson's plane crashed on the last night of 1985. They drank beer from coolers, passed joints, tried to turn the music loud enough to fill that empty field and the long silence surrounding it. Beneath whatever moon there was and stars shifting too slowly to track, they felt themselves more alive in a place where others had fallen. Graves and the stone monuments cast for the dead are one thing. The places they fell are another, small territories granted mystery because a treasured spirit vanished there. As though some danger may linger, as though blood lost there might rise from the dirt and stain one's feet. In the town where Dixon and I went to school, one guitar shop had a small museum of stringed instruments attached. Some of Rick Nelson's guitars and hand-tooled guitar straps hung there beside an antique banjo, a string bass carved from a cedar trunk, a three-necked mandolin. A sign warned not to touch the instruments. A rule I broke only once, when I thumbed the unturned E string of one of Nelson's guitars, then stood listening while the plump note resonated far longer than it should, a voice willing itself to go on.

The Day Patty Hearst Was Captured

The band that sang "Up against the wall" and proclaimed
"gotta revolution" renamed themselves and crooned
that if only you believed like they believed you wouldn't know
the noise, the light-splotched film of Saigon falling,
the last helicopter lumbering up from the embassy roof,

rising in smoke-grained sky, the fingers of the final refugees
peeling from the skids, bodies dropping into the fate
of crowds. Every record collection on the street contained
a copy of *Rumours,* whether anyone remembered buying it
or not. Nixon slept in San Clemente. Everybody burned one

on the way to work or school and sang without listening
to the radio. Good weather once made revolution
and robbing banks more fun than school, no matter whether
you lived with the math teacher or not. That was last year,
when small armies still commandeered the front page.

Now everyone just wants to drop a 'lude and dance.
All the bands are cutting their disco tracks, transgressions
more lucrative than holdups, unlikely to startle anyone
to tommy gun justice. The girl at Burger King gave me
too much change. I have not looked at a paper in weeks.

And underneath the collected noise of every house around me
spinning the same record, someone could put on a new shirt,
change a name and move, not free like the records released
five years ago screamed "free," but unencumbered
by suspicions or second looks. But if everyone listens

to the same record, the same silence falls at the end.
I'm spending my windfall change on jukeboxes and pinball.
And this morning a mist came like breath-smoke
from the tall grass in empty lots and men climbed old stairs
to capture the answer to questions no one is asking.

Vulture Skull

I found the bird in a field shorn
by harvest, dead and already broken
among the stalky remains of beans,
cotton, whatever the season planted.
Under the circle its brothers made,
I cut the head from the body,
surprised how easily they separated,
took it home to nest on a shelf
above my desk. When I picked it up,
I never saw bird, field, angled plain
of sky, but dark weaving through
the tunnels and chambers in bone,
the same dark vultures seek
when they spear into flesh, dark
that hosts both what is foul in us
and any spark of infinity we might own.
Light does not rise. The body, extinguished,
offers little in the way of enlightenment.
But in that balsa-weight skull
lay the seeds of prayer or song,
something to lift us above
the weight of bone for
a few breaths before appetite
pulls us once more to earth.

In the Poetry Museum

You will pause before the time-honored
    and shimmering as you must
        and as you are intended,

before you begin your solitary way, delighted
    with the odor of ink flowering
        in your nostrils, the gravity

of paper determined not to become ash and dirt.
    You can follow the guided crowds a while
        before seeking the smaller chambers

whose ill-fitting exhibits are haunted
    by fierce acolytes, fire-warped believers.
        You can linger a long time, can linger

a whole life in the discipline of those rooms.
    But to know this place, finally
        you must descend the stairwell

that takes you to the halls under the halls, home
    to the materials never assimilated
        into exhibitions. Those corridors,

invisible as bones, burnished by the shuffling
    of the curious before you, lie choked
        with books, with pages torn

from books, with incomplete histories of apocalypse
    and resurrection. Light grows irregular
        down here. Bulbs startle into life,

then blink shut. The smell rising to your nostrils, old,
      thick, defies scansion or armatures
            of rhyme. Many turn back here,

afraid what mirrors might present themselves,
      what self-portraits must be drawn
            in the dust. This is when

one remembers the root of "verse" means "to turn."
      To turn, but not retreat. To continue
            is to risk smaller hallways

where you must bend to enter, where you carry
      your own light and walk floors cracking
            to rubble, places where you might step

in mud or worse. Iambs of water plop around you.
      Papers mingle with earth until print
            and dirt become one

unreadable substance. Down here, you discover
      that monuments rise on the foundations
            of failures, and you learn the virtue

of the attempt. This will be the lesson that brings you
      back to a world selective in its deafness,
            where, with hands empty and ink-scarred,

you join the ongoing and incomplete enterprise.

Sleeping Through the Graveyard Shift

Last night I dreamed of work again, going
        where I had no desire to go, webs of sleep
still sweeping from my body as I ascended
        tall ladders, temples pulsing with
gas station coffee. In the dream, I knew the routine
        though things kept happening to disrupt
the machine rhythm workers fall into.

The dream's plot, as always, was arbitrary, fragments
        of image and word flashing with the weary
insistence of a Christmas tree in February. Mine
        was not the labor-dream of Joe Hill, who died
saying, "Don't mourn, organize," or Eugene Debs,
        leader of the dreaming Wobblies. My dreams
sing no labor songs, carry no union cards.

I woke, still shackled to those fragments, the apron
        mapped with blood, the hallway could be
from one of my schools. Maybe this meant
        work was one of my educators. I spent years
working the algebra of shovels, cash registers ringing
        the Karl Marx waltz. In one dream, I teach,
in another I pour concrete, load a truck in the rain.

It's always the same job, endless, its one design
        to provoke rage and leave the body deeper poverty
than it owned upon waking. But the job
        I woke up from continues, its quotas stuttering
and faulty equipment fractures. Light fixtures fall
        and shatter as the boss yells we're all working
late, no room for sleep until this is all done.

Old Records

Because they are unwritten chapters
of autobiography, not mine alone
but yours or anyone's who ever went
into a room to listen to music alone,
whose ponytailed or dog-collared friends
hooted at the Gordon Lightfoot
or Carole King kept deep in the stack
to play when no one was around,
                              because
they were too fragile to maintain,
their patterns of scratches and dust
marking each record with its own
collection of competing noise,
                         because
I would save lunch money to buy
records filled with songs
I had not heard,
                 each one was
a universe, two-sided, incandescent.

A steel needle muscled through
the grooves of the $1.49 album I bought
at Colonial Grocery, a grab bag
of artists—Lulu, Mark Lindsay,
Pacific Gas and Electric, Santana—signed
to Columbia, its sleeve
standard issue psychedelia, all of it
slapped together with no sense
of how song fit into song.

I played it
as obsessively as NASA's scientists tried
to hear patterns in space dust and noise
to see if anything out there wanted
to speak with us. By then, Woolworth's,
the furniture store, the five and dime all
offered a rack of records as it became clear
music sold more easily than end tables,
more consistently than white socks
or tricycles.
                    Impossible to say everything
songs promise, so I will not,
but understand—
                    we carried them
with us, imagining them
when we could not hear them
in those days before iPods
or the now-vanished Walkman or phones
that dialed in songs from the air.
And like all things imagined,
they grew perfect.
                    I have compact discs,
hard drives crowded with songs,
more music than a lifetime
will absorb,
                    and I love none of it
more than I loved that tilted stack
of records, the edges
of their cardboard jackets dissolving,
the needle skimming the first fat groove
to grind out the opening notes,
the thinning voices that sang
through the dust of this one imperfect universe
and all the ones still to come.

Where I Was

We have never spoken of those mornings
    when the singular blessing of the unmovable
cold was how quickly it dispersed whiskey fumes
    from the night before. The truck's heater huffed
and coughed but never quite worked, and fingers
    went numb around Styrofoam cups
of coffee that would not be emptied before
    we arrived for another day of battering
frozen earth, coaxing steel, concrete
    and wood to take shape, to rise and hold.
Now, buildings rise without us, and we say
    nothing of what it costs to live like that,
but sometimes I stop the car and stare a while
    as a concrete truck backs up to a pour
or a crane flies a load to the top slab
    of a high rise, and I reach again
into the empty pockets and hard sleep
    of a life that didn't want me to remember
or write down a single word, and touch again
    the cold still ready to hold me.

Zero Gravity

Wayne Shorter Quartet, February 11, 2011

Delivered by Mapquest, by GPS, directed
    by passengers who came here for other shows,
the guilts and worries we shoulder through the door
    are not absolved, but briefly abandoned
inside the turns, the calls and response of this music
    that winds and stutters, that refuses to resolve,
always reminding us that this concert,
    these seats are a pause, not a destination.
In front of me, a woman leans her head against
    a man's shoulder, then jerks upright,
quivering at this new exchange: the drums snap
    a cadence, the piano suggests softer weather.
The bass asks and repeats its single question.
    And we forget protests in the Middle East,
the rising cost of gasoline, the songs we expected
    to hear in the lifting of one long chord
Shorter blows, the other three still for a second
    before they start forward like hikers who woke
to find maps gone, landmarks erased, even stars
    invisible, leaving them nothing but faith
in the way forward. When the music falls,
    as it will, to silence, the musicians will wave
from the stage and vanish, leaving us winter,
    the lives waiting outside the door,
the sky's silent canopy and the stars, whose end
    we will never see, slowly burning visible.

The Piano As a City

From the galleries and downtown clubs of middle C, some walk into the old neighborhoods where every house has a front porch. A few dwellings sit empty, keys that stick or ring an unturned note, and some widows still wearing black stay in the long shadows of memory, offer the corner kids peppermints that taste of dust and spiders. In the wide and windy estates of the bass clef, great houses stay shuttered and locked and nothing moves but light. The sidewalks of the upper registers crack and narrow and it gets hard to take any word seriously. But down the street from the dog-trot school, a man has opened his worn book of prayers and, half-reading half-improvising, has begun to harangue the traffic, the dust-anchored wind. His most fervent prayer is that his voice carries, soaks into the scraped tiles of the school, the mortar dissolving between the bricks, the gleaming tables a bartender towels an hour before the drinkers arrive. He sets a brandy snifter on the piano for tips, knowing the piano player will arrive hung over and will not think of it until his second drink. Afternoons like this, clouds washing over the sun, the sky empty of all desire, the city feels like a hymn, one chord in the great unwritten symphony. When you walk, every step echoes a voice from another part of the city as sidewalk bleeds into sidewalk, as streets erase into the grind of lawnmowers, the hum of barber's clippers, the cadences of old air-conditioners and window fans. The black panes in the windows of shut-down stores track you. Today I want to walk through every note and chord this city offers, until I can become part of the chorus that arises beyond note and chord, beyond what can be written or even heard but must be felt. Those windy anarchies that make people open their doors and walk slowly onto the sidewalks until, slowly, a brave few begin to dance under traffic lights that continue their timed changes though no cars are moving this great weather of sound.

Hard Luck: A Requiem for Jerry Quarry

1.

First, the fist. The flat-knuckled hand, work scarred, lettered with
        India ink and a sewing needle, a letter on each finger

so his fists spelled *Hard Luck,* mantra for the low punches
        and cheap shots life deals out. The busted straight,

the dice that come up snake eyes, bad jobs, aching knees. Layoffs.
        All the small rages channeled into teaching his sons

to set their feet and throw a punch. Balance.
        The blow coming through the body, the next hit

coming from another angle, grinding his opponent's will
        into the sand no sweeping could clean from a plank floor.

"There's no quit in a Quarry," the old man reminds them
        until they believe it, breathe it, carry it

into rings all over the world, saving their fiercest fighting
        for one another, their sparring sessions stopping

all activity in the gym giving each other scars they carry under
        hard lights where they bleed and prove the old man right.

2.

My last vision of him, in the unyielding glare of a camera,
      as he shuffled, spoke in the broken syllables

of a man who has survived something horrible he can't recall,
      unwound the videos I've spent hours watching:

Jerry Quarry stalking the ring, never backing up, waiting
      for his opponent to make a mistake, patient

even when Ali or Frazier beats him to the punch,
      draws blood and slips the counter-punch.

In one video, the worn film stock overexposed and stained by light,
      the shot flickers as though time is sanding

the two fighters into chimeras, names released from bodies
      to become pure legend, like the unfilmed fighters

of centuries gone: John L. Sullivan, Peter Jackson.
      Quarry comes through wavering light, waiting until

one of his body hooks bends the other boxer. Then
      his hands fly like a drummer's, beating

the savage melody that is soundtrack to man's oldest sport.

3.

Too slow for games that required speed, too weak
      to supply power, I was left to prove my worth

in the improvisations of after school fights. Enough of those
      and you gain a little prowess, learn that pain

and blood end but end nothing. I knew that when I walked
      into the damp basement, its air curdled with sweat

and dead cigarette smoke of the old men who watched us
      flail each other and spit or grumbled directions

we couldn't hear or follow. Blood wouldn't end
      the sparring, but tears would.

The first night I was fed to someone older and meaner,
      whose job it was to make sure I didn't come back.

But Jerry Quarry's endless stamina had marked me,
      so I came back and spent the next few weeks

sparring with a kid more or less my size two or three
      nights a week. Neither of us inflicted or sustained

much damage, but we kept on, understanding
      the one who didn't come back first was the loser.

Some nights, leaving, I read the clippings in a glass case,
      aged tobacco-brown, brittle with age, triumphs of boys

better than we were, better than we could ever be.
      Next to one clipping, the obituary of a boy in uniform.

4.

Jerry Quarry was the single fighter to say yes when
        Muhammad Ali returned from suspension and needed

someone to fight. Since part of America had always wished for
        a great white hope in the ring and longed especially

for one to take out a draft dodger from the Nation of Islam,
        a red-headed hooking machine with Irish blood was made

to order. The fight was in Atlanta, an hour from us, but
        my dad stopped giving a rat's ass about boxing

before I was born. By then I'd given up sparring in the basement.
        If I wanted a fight, they were easy to find, but I'd been hit

and hit back enough to know that respect purchased by
        trading fists is not respect, and winning fights has nothing

to do with justice. Even though I suspected Ali got a raw deal
        and Vietnam was no place to die, I pulled for Quarry

out of habit or respect. Who knows? The fight went the way
        of many of Quarry's fights in the 70s—he took

too many punches, began to bleed, and the fight was called.
        "He always cut too easy," Joe Frazier said years later.

5.

Hard luck. A phrase used to explain and excuse
　　　　so much of Quarry's career. The words tattooed

across the old man's knuckles, the hairline split
　　　　of scar tissue over one eye, then the other.

The first letters I ever saw tattooed on a hand
　　　　were on a boy who appeared in eighth grade,

just back from training school, he told us. One hand, still
　　　　a boy's soft fist, was lettered *Love,* the other *Hate.*

By the time I figured out training school was prison
　　　　for those too young for prison, he was gone

though I'd see him walking here or there
　　　　over the next couple of years, wasting time before

he vanished like he was never there at all,
　　　　the way those letters faded into the dirt

of the body, the words little scars to mark
　　　　the boy who once lived in that body.

6.

For Jack Butler

The photograph was taped over my bed for so long
      I might have stopped seeing it: a page from *Sports Illustrated*,

Quarry fighting Jimmy Ellis. Quarry was taking a punch,
      his face twisted by the impact, his gloved fist lifted

to strike. He would lose this fight, his first shot
      at the heavyweight title. That picture stayed,

a flash of color like the picture I saved of Jimi Hendrix
      burning his guitar, those two photos bright planets

in a universe of black and white photographs of bands
      scowling from doorways, cemeteries, city streets,

a collection of glooms. Maybe that photograph taught me
      to love the ones who keep coming, whose art

is perseverance: the graveyard waitress, the hot tar roofer,
      the pitcher who takes the mound after being knocked out

of his last three games, the writer finishing his sixth
      unpublished novel, the band grinding through one more

rendition of a song popular in 1978, the concrete finisher,
      anyone willing to bear the scars of a day's demands.

7.

I hadn't made an angry fist in a decade
        when I saw Jerry Quarry on TV, stooping

as he walked, his words a stumbling slur. He needed help
        to get dressed, to eat, as each blow he'd taken

echoed again, reclaiming a little more of what it took.
        Twenty years after what should have been his last fight—

he kept sneaking back to the ring like a man unwilling
        to let an old lover go—he was a palsied vessel,

lifting his fists again for the cameras.
        No words were lettered there, but in their rising

the old man said again, "There's no quit
        in a Quarry," a motto engraved in his son's flesh

deeper than any ink, any blow could ever reach.

Acknowledgments

No book ends up in a reader's hands by itself. I want to thank my friends Roy Bentley, Suzanne Cleary, and Adam Tavel for reading earlier drafts of these poems.

I also need to give a shout out to Malcolm Holcombe, Alan Kaufman, R.B. Morris, and the late David Olney, my friends in The Liberty Circus.

A big thanks to Sandy Longhorn whose artwork provided the cover. Thanks to Robert Canipe and Tim Peeler at Redhawk Publications and Redhawk Creative Solutions. I will be forever grateful to you for reaching out. And to all of those I have not named whose friendship sustains me.

And to Jamie and Isabel. Without them, nothing is possible.

About the Author

 Al Maginnes was born in Massachusetts and grew up in a number of states, mostly in the southeast. He has degrees in English and writing from East Carolina University and the University of Arkansas. Al is the author of seven full length collections of poetry, as well as a number of chapbooks. He is music editor of the online journal *Connotation*. After more than thirty years of teaching, he has retired and currently teaches workshops and does some freelance writing.